Date Due

FEB 21		
MAR 3 0		
JUL 3 1 1968		
APR. 19 1972		
ⓖ PRINTED IN U. S. A.		

THE BOOK OF
REVELATION

Uniform with this volume

LETTERS TO YOUNG CHURCHES
(*The New Testament Epistles*)

THE GOSPELS IN MODERN ENGLISH

THE YOUNG CHURCH IN ACTION
(*The Acts of the Apostles*)

translated by J. B. PHILLIPS

THE BOOK OF
REVELATION

A new translation of the Apocalypse

by

J. B. PHILLIPS

New York
THE MACMILLAN COMPANY
1957

To all those hopeful and encouraging
people who for many years have urged
me to undertake this work

TRANSLATOR'S PREFACE

THE BOOK of Revelation, entitled in the King James Version "The Revelation of Saint John the Divine," was probably originally entitled "A Revelation of John." Books of revelation, or apocalypses, were common in Jewish literature in times of national persecution, and this Christian apocalypse closely follows the form and style of such writings. Yet the claim made at the very beginning of the book is startling and unique—it is no less than "a Revelation from Jesus Christ, which God gave Him," and which was disclosed to John through an angelic intermediary. Although there was much argument and hesitation before this book was established within the canon of the New Testament, the historic fact is that from about the fifth century onward the Western Churches at least accepted this book as uniquely inspired. I have therefore felt justified in giving this translation of the work the title of *The Book of Revelation*.

Although the majority of Christians quite cheerfully accept the inclusion of this mysterious book within the New Testament canon, my strong impression is that very few of them have read it in any detail. Most Christians, for example, are familiar with the Messages to the Seven Churches contained in the first three chapters, and know something of the closing two chapters of the book with their strangely haunting visions of the Holy City, the New Heaven and the new earth, and the strong promises of God to the faithful believer. But the intervening chapters remain puzzling and baffling to many sincere Christians. The form and idiom of apocalyptic writing are exceedingly strange to modern minds, and while the queer visions provide every opportunity for the diversion of cranks and fanatics, the sober Christian soon finds himself at a loss to understand, and in consequence frequently neglects the book completely.

I was naturally tempted to omit this book altogether from my translational work, a course, incidentally, taken by Calvin in his New Testament commentary. But this would lead to the obvious implication that I was taking it upon myself to exclude this work from the New Testament! Admittedly there have been times when I have sympathized with Martin Luther in his declaration that this book is "neither apostolic nor prophetic," that "everyone thinks of the book whatever his spirit suggests," and even "that there are many nobler books to be retained." Yet after much study I became satisfied that the Christian Church was justified in including this book in the Sacred Canon.

Eventually I began the translation of this book for two reasons, and I think that the results of my work may prove surprising. My first and obvious reason for doing the work at all is that I naturally wanted to complete my study, as well as my translation, of the whole New Testament. Like many another Christian I knew this book only superficially. My hope was that just as the essential truth of the Gospels and Epistles sprang to fresh life in the process of translation, so new truth and understanding would break upon me as I attempted to turn this peculiar Greek into modern English. This hope has not been altogether fulfilled, partly because my own method of translation, which is suitable enough for the narrative of the Gospels and the Acts, and to the epistolary style of Paul and the others, does not appear to lend itself to translating language which is both symbolic and poetic, and which could easily lose both beauty and significance when reduced to a workaday vocabulary.

Nevertheless it soon became clear that, although the task was not the same as it had been in the other parts of the New Testament, it could prove useful and even, in the true sense of that threadbare word, thrilling. For in this book the translator is carried into another dimension—he has but the slightest foothold in the time-and-space world with which he is familiar. He is carried, not into some never-never land of fancy, but into the ever-ever land of God's eternal Values and Judgments. It is true that the expressions are often conventionally apocalyptic, but the translator can hardly fail to sense the urgency of the Seer as he tries to express the inexpressible. Surely something of the sense of timelessness, the feeling of the supramundane, can be conveyed. At least the language can be freed from archaisms and some verbal obscurities, and made more like that which a modern mystic might wish to use in setting down a series of burning instants of Heavenly vision.

As the character of the task became clearer to me I thought of my second reason for undertaking the translation—which is simply that a great many people have written asking me to do so! I think that for them, as for me, there lies something of a surprise. For I am pretty sure that those who found the obscurities of Paul's Epistles dissipated by the plain English of *Letters to Young Churches* will expect the obscurities of the book of Revelation to be dispersed by the same method. But quite plainly the cause of obscurity in Paul's letters is not the same as in John's apocalypse. In the case of Paul there is rarely any real doubt as to what his original intention was, complicated and compressed though his expressions sometimes are. It is comparatively easy, by using imaginative insight, a little expansion, and occasionally a little paraphrase, to turn into modern English his inspired thoughts of nearly two thousand years ago. But in the book of Revelation the obscurity is of a different and much more impenetrable quality. Who can truly translate unless he is quite sure of the original meaning? Who can explain or expand if both mystery and compression are felt to be an essential part of the original writing? If the author intends a mystery, then the translator must transmit a mystery; if the author is deliberately obscure the translator can only reproduce the obscurity!

If, then, my friends who have written to me so encouragingly and hopefully are expecting the sort of detailed explanation which only a commentary can supply, or speculate about, they will not find it here in this work of translation. I must simply refer them to the Commentaries listed. But if they will read the whole of this mysterious book in the English of today, and allow its awe-inspiring sweep and compass to affect them as it affected me, they may be surprised but I do not think they will be disappointed.

*   *   *

Now although I do not possess the special knowledge required in a commentator on apocalyptic, I feel it is legitimate and indeed might prove useful to record something of my impressions as a translator. The most obvious and striking feature of the book at first sight is the oddness of the Greek in which it is written. The differences of style and composition between the various books of the New Testament are completely hidden for most English readers by the over-all majesty of the King James Version. (Indeed, it is doubtful whether any difference in the style of writing between any of the New Testament books could be detected if one worked from the King James Version alone. The actual difference in style between, let us say, Luke's Gospel and Paul's Epistle to the Romans is very marked and, like other modern translators, I have made some attempt to reproduce this difference in the mode of translation.) But when one is confronted with the language of Revelation it is no mere difference of style which makes one gasp, but crudities, grammatical errors, and a quite extraordinary juxtaposition of words. So wholly different is the book in its word usage and composition from the Fourth Gospel that many scholars find themselves unable to believe that both could be written by the same person. The Fourth Gospel is written, within its limited vocabulary, smoothly and correctly and would probably have caused no literary qualms in a contemporary Greek reader. But Revelation piles word upon word remorselessly, mixes cases and tenses without apparent scruple, and shows at times a complete disregard for normal syntax and grammar. Here, for example, are a few words from Chapter 8, Verse 13, translated literally, representing roughly the appearance such Greek would present to an educated reader of the first century:

> And I saw, and I heard one eagle flying in midheaven
> saying in a loud voice,
> "Alas, alas, alas for the inhabitants upon the earth
> from the remaining voices of the trumpet of the three
> angels about to sound the trumpet!"

And such an example could be multiplied again and again. But, generally speaking, the tumultuous assault of words is not without its effect upon the mind, although I must confess I find it very difficult to believe that such a surprising attack could have been deliberately engineered. The inspired words seem to me to pour forth in a stream both uninhibited

and uncorrected, and I therefore find it impossible to agree
with those who say that this work is either a revision of an
earlier one or a combination of several such works. The
writer's mind was plainly steeped in the spirit and in the
knowledge of Jewish apocalyptic. There is hardly a single
direct quotation from the Old Testament, but there are
scores of parallels, echoes, and recollections of it. John's
words give the strong impression of one whose thoughts and
thought forms are Hebrew, and yet it is a puzzle to understand why such a keen and intelligent mind could not read-
ily have mastered the simple usages of New Testament
Greek. I make therefore this bold suggestion: the writer, who
had a genuine ecstatic experience, wrote down what he saw
during the visions. The intense emotion of being, as it were,
"in the heavenlies," the excitement of seeing what is nor-
mally invisible to human eyes, and the frustration of having
to use human words to describe what is beyond human ex-
pression would, it seems to me, fully account for the incoher-
ence, the strange formation of sentences, the repetition, and
the odd juxtaposition of words. If we suppose this to be true,
and if we suppose also that the writer were wholly convinced
that what he had written was in fact written while "in the
spirit," then we can reasonably imagine that he would shrink
from correction or revision lest he distort or modify the
revelation he had been given.

I feel I must record that, once one has absorbed the initial
shock of the peculiar Greek, the effect of the language of
this book is most powerful. The crowns, the thrones, the
gold, the jewels, the colors, the trumpets, the violence of
action and the impact of incredible numbers and awe-inspiring size—all these images stir that threshold of the brain
where monsters lurk and supernatural glories blaze. John is

stirring with a kind of surrealistic artistry the vastnesses of our unconscious minds. The book is probably an impossibility for the pictorial illustrator, but the figures created in the mind are vivid and powerful enough to transport us to another spiritual dimension. Once we are gripped by the mysterious compulsion of these visions we find the "silence in Heaven for what seemed to be about half an hour" almost intolerable. The "solitary eagle flying in midheaven," crying out in pity for the inhabitants of the earth is, out of its context, bizarre to the point of absurdity, but, set as it is, it is almost unbearably poignant. And how beautifully right, how poetically satisfying it is to read that the leaves of the Tree of Life in the New Jerusalem are for the healing of the nations! The poetic impact of the book carries us away to a realm where the pedestrian rules of grammar no longer apply—we are dealing with celestial poetry and not with earthly prose. To be literal-minded and studiously analytical in such a work is to kill its poetic truth. Dissection is not infrequently the death of beauty.

I am conscious, then, of not having done much beyond removing some of the obscurities of archaic language. If there is any truth in my surmise that John was reluctant to alter or improve the messages he wrote down in ecstasy, then the reader will understand my own even greater reluctance to demolish the high poetry of these strange utterances by reducing them to the language of everyday experience. Almost any poem can be made to look ridiculous by having its superficial meaning reduced to ordinary prose. (We have only thus to "translate" Keats's "Ode on a Grecian Urn" or Shelley's "To a Skylark" to see how easily the magic and mystery can be destroyed!) This by no means proves that a poem is bad poetry; on the contrary it emphasizes the proper use of poetry which, by indefinable subtleties of rhythm, rhyme, and cadence, can strike chords and overtones forever beyond the reach of the finest prose. Consequently my earnest hope is that the use of modern language has not quenched the flame which blazes through this magnificently ecstatic poem of the Majesty and Sovereignty of God.

SWANAGE, DORSET   J. B. PHILLIPS
   1956

THE BOOK OF REVELATION

AUTHOR: *John the Apostle, John the Elder or another lead-ing Christian by the name of John.*

(Justin Martyr in his "Dialogue with Trypho the Jew," written about 140, appears to ascribe the authorship of this book to John the Apostle. But Dionysius, Bishop of Alexan-dria from 249 to 265, a learned and holy man, could not accept John the Apostle as the author of this Revelation, and gave almost conclusive reasons for his opinion. Since those early days there has been much argument, and much re-search has gone into the problem of establishing authorship but without conclusive result. It is essential that the reader should study a good commentary on the subject of author-ship, so that he may appreciate the difficulties involved. Some books are listed on pages 49 and 50.)

DATE: *Probably about 95, but some hold to an earlier date.*

DESTINATION: *This book is plainly intended primarily for the Seven Churches of Asia. But since the Message of the book is relevant to all Christians under persecution, and since the book treats of Divine Judgments upon the whole world, the author must surely have intended it to be circulated among all Christian communities.*

THEME: *This book consists of a series of visions granted to John while in exile for his Christian witness. The language is highly symbolic and figurative; and attempts in modern days to fit its prophecies into contemporary situations have led interpreters into all kinds of difficulties. It is thought by many that the symbols and figures of the book would be understood by the Christians to whom the book was first sent, but that the key to their interpretation has now been lost. However, certain themes emerge distinctly for the modern reader's profit:*

1. The absolute sovereignty of God, and His ultimate purpose to destroy all forms of evil.

2. The inevitable judgments of God upon evil, upon the worship of false gods, which include riches, power, and success.

3. The necessity for patient endurance, the ultimate security being the knowledge that God is in control of history.

4. The existence of reality, represented here under such symbols as the New Jerusalem, apart and secure from the battles and tribulations of earthly life, promises complete spiritual security to those who are faithful to God and His Christ.

5. The glimpses of worship and adoration, constantly offered to God and the Lamb, are a kind of pattern of man's ultimate acknowledgment of the Character of God when he sees Him as He is.

But for any proper appreciation of the themes of this mysterious book it is imperative that the reader should make use of one or more commentaries.

SPECIAL NOTE: *The Greek of this book is peculiar in construction and is occasionally ungrammatical. Sometimes, in the visions, for instance, there is a mixing of past and present tenses. After careful consideration the translator has decided not to reproduce these oddities, except where a sudden change of tense adds vividness to the description.*

THE REVELATION OF JOHN

CONCERNING THIS BOOK

This is a Revelation from Jesus Christ, which God gave Him so that He might show His servants what must very soon take place. He made it known by sending His angel to His servant John, who is the witness of all that he saw—the Message of God, and the Testimony of Jesus Christ.

Happy is the man who reads this prophecy and happy are those who hear it read and pay attention to its Message; for the time is short.

JOHN'S GREETING AND ASCRIPTION

John, to the Seven Churches in Asia:

Grace and peace be to you from Him Who is and Who was and Who is coming, from the Seven Spirits before His Throne, and from Jesus Christ the faithful Witness, First-Born of the dead, and Ruler of kings upon earth. To Him Who loves us and has set us free from our sins through His own blood, Who has made us a kingdom of priests to His God and Father, to Him be glory and power for timeless ages, Amen!

See, He is coming in the clouds and every eye shall see

Him, even those who pierced Him, and His coming will mean bitter sorrow to every tribe upon the earth. So let it be!

"I am Alpha and Omega," says the Lord God, "Who is and Who was and Who is coming, the Almighty."

THE MESSAGE TO THE SEVEN CHURCHES

1
9
    I, John, who am your brother and your companion in the distress, the kingdom and the faithful endurance to which Jesus calls us, was on the island called Patmos because I had spoken God's Message and borne witness to Jesus. On the Lord's Day I knew myself inspired by the Spirit, and I heard from behind me a voice loud as a trumpet call, saying,

"Write down in a book what you see, and send it to the Seven Churches—to Ephesus, Smyrna, Pergamum, Thyatira, Sardis, Philadelphia and Laodicea!"

I turned to see whose voice it was that was speaking to me, and when I had turned I saw seven golden lampstands, and among these lampstands I saw someone like a Son of Man. He was dressed in a long robe with a golden girdle around His breast; His head and His hair were white as snow-white wool, His eyes blazed like fire, and His feet shone as the finest bronze glows in the furnace. His voice had the sound of a great waterfall, and I saw that in His right hand He held seven stars. A sharp two-edged sword came out of His mouth, and His face was ablaze like the sun at its height.

When my eyes took in this sight I fell at His feet like a dead man. And then He placed His right hand upon me and said:

"Do not be afraid. I am the First and the Last, the Living One. I am He Who was dead, and now you see Me alive for timeless ages! I hold in My hand the keys of Death and the Grave. Therefore, write down what you have seen, both the

things which are now, and the things which are to be here-
after. The secret meaning of the seven stars which you saw
in My right hand, and of the seven golden lampstands is this:
The seven stars are the angels of the seven Churches and the
seven lampstands are the Churches themselves."

(1) TO THE LOVELESS CHURCH

"Write this to the angel of the Church in Ephesus: 2

"These words are spoken by the One Who holds the seven   1
stars safe in His right hand, and Who walks among the seven
golden lampstands. I know what you have done; I know how
hard you have worked and what you have endured. I know
that you will not tolerate wicked men, that you have put to
the test self-styled 'Apostles,' who are nothing of the sort,
and have found them to be liars. I know your powers of
endurance—how you have suffered for the sake of My
Name and have not grown weary. But I hold this against you,
that you do not love as you did at first. Remember how far
you have fallen. Repent and live as you lived at first. Other-
wise, if your heart remains unchanged, I shall come to you
and remove your lampstand from its place.

"Yet you have this to your credit, that you hate the prac-   2
tices of the Nicolaitans, which I Myself detest. Let every   6
listener hear what the Spirit says to the Churches:

"To the victorious I will give the right to eat from the
Tree of Life which grows in the Paradise of God."

(2) TO THE PERSECUTED CHURCH

"Write this to the angel of the Church in Smyrna: 2

"These words are spoken by the First and the Last, Who   8
died and came to life again. I know of your tribulation and
of your poverty—though in fact you are rich! I know how

you are slandered by those who call themselves Jews, but in fact are no Jews but a synagogue of Satan. Have no fear of what you will suffer. I tell you now that the Devil is going to cast some of your number into prison where your faith will be tested and your distress will last for ten days. Be faithful in the face of death and I will give you the crown of life. Let every listener hear what the Spirit says to the Churches:

"The victorious cannot suffer the slightest hurt from the Second Death."

(3) TO THE OVER-TOLERANT CHURCH

2   "Write this to the angel of the Church in Pergamum:

12   "These words are spoken by Him Who has the sharp two-edged sword. I know where you live—where Satan sits enthroned. I know that you hold fast to My Name and that you never denied your faith in Me even in the days when Antipas, My faithful witness, was martyred before your eyes in the very house of Satan.

"Yet I have a few things against you—some of your number cling to the teaching of Balaam, the man who taught Balak how to entice the children of Israel into eating meat sacrificed to idols and into sexual immorality. I have also against you the fact that among your number are some who hold just as closely to the teaching of the Nicolaitans. Repent, then, or else I shall come to you quickly and make war upon them with the sword of My mouth. Let the listener hear what the Spirit says to the Churches:

"I will give the victorious some of the hidden manna, and I will also give him a white stone with a new name written upon it which no man knows except the man who receives it."

(4) TO THE COMPROMISING CHURCH

"Write this to the angel of the Church in Thyatira: 2

"These are the words of the Son of God Whose eyes   18
blaze like fire and Whose feet shine like the finest bronze:

"I know what you have done. I know of your love and
your loyalty, your service and your endurance. Moreover,
I know that you are doing more than you did at first. But I
have this against you, that you tolerate that Jezebel-woman
who calls herself a prophetess, but who by her teaching deceives my servants into sexual immorality and eating idols'-
meat. I have given her time to repent but she has shown no
desire to repent of her immorality. See, now, how I throw her
into bed and her lovers with her, and I will send them terri-
ble suffering unless they repent of what she has done. As
for her children, I shall strike them dead. Then all the
Churches will know that I am the One Who searches men's
hearts and minds, and that I will reward each one of you
according to your deeds.

"But for the rest of you at Thyatira, who do not hold
this teaching, and have not learned what they call 'the deep
things of Satan,' I will lay no further burden upon you.
Hold on to what you have until I come!

"To the one who is victorious, who carries out My work
to the end, I will give authority over the nations, just as I
Myself have received authority from My Father, and I will
give him the morning star. He shall 'shepherd them with a
rod of iron'; he shall 'dash them in pieces like a potter's vessel.' Let the listener hear what the Spirit says to the
Churches."

(5) TO THE SLEEPING CHURCH

3   "Write this to the angel of the Church in Sardis:

1   "These are the words of Him Who holds in His hand the seven Spirits of God and the seven stars:

"I know what you have done, that you have a reputation for being alive, but that in fact you are dead. Now wake up! Strengthen what you still have before it dies! For I have not found any of your deeds complete in the sight of My God. Remember then what you were given and what you were taught. Hold to those things and repent. If you refuse to wake up, then I will come to you like a thief, and you will have no idea of the hour of My coming.

"Yet you still have a few names in Sardis of people who have not soiled their garments. They shall walk with Me in white, for they have deserved to do so. The victorious shall wear such white garments, and never will I erase his name from the Book of Life. Indeed, I will speak his name openly before My Father and His angels. Let the listener hear what the Spirit says to the Churches."

(6) TO THE CHURCH WITH OPPORTUNITY

3   "Then write this to the angel of the Church in Phila-
7   delphia:

"These are the words of the Holy One and the True, Who holds the key of David, Who opens and no man shall shut, and Who shuts and no man shall open. I know what you have done. See, I have given you a door flung wide open, which no man can close! For you have some little power and have been faithful to My Message and have not denied My Name. See how I deal with those of Satan's synagogue, who claim to be Jews, yet are no Jews but liars!

Watch how I make them come and bow down before your feet and acknowledge that I have loved you. Because you have obeyed My call to patient endurance I will keep you safe from the hour of trial which is to come upon the whole world, to test all who live upon the earth. I am coming soon; hold fast to what you have—let no one deprive you of your crown. As for the victorious, I will make him a pillar in the Temple of My God, and he will never leave it. I will write upon him the Name of My God, and the name of the City of My God, the New Jerusalem which comes down out of Heaven from My God. And I will write upon him My own new Name. Let the listener hear what the Spirit says to the Churches."

(7)   TO THE COMPLACENT CHURCH

"Then write this to the angel of the Church in Laodicea: 3
"These are the words of the Amen, the faithful and true   14
Witness, the Beginning of God's Creation:

"I know what you have done, and that you are neither cold nor hot. I could wish that you were either cold or hot! But since you are lukewarm and neither hot nor cold, I intend to spit you out of my mouth! While you say, 'I am rich, I have prospered, and there is nothing that I need,' you have no eyes to see that you are wretched, pitiable, poverty-stricken, blind and naked. My advice to you is to buy from Me that gold which is purified in the furnace so that you may be rich, and white garments to wear so that you may hide the shame of your nakedness, and salve to put on your eyes to make you see. All those whom I love I correct and discipline. Therefore, shake off your complacency and repent. See, I stand knocking at the door. If anyone listens to My Voice and opens the door, I will go into his house and dine with him, and he with Me. As for the victorious, I will give him the honor of sitting beside Me on My Throne, just as I Myself have won the victory and have taken My seat beside My Father on His Throne. Let the listener hear what the Spirit says to the Churches."

THE VISION OF HEAVEN

4
1   Later I looked again, and before my eyes a door stood open in Heaven, and in my ears was the voice with the ring of a trumpet, which I had heard at first, speaking to me and saying,

"Come up here, and I will show you what must happen in the future."

Immediately I knew myself to be inspired by the Spirit, and in my vision I saw that a Throne had been set up in Heaven, and there was someone seated upon the Throne. His appearance blazed like diamond and topaz, and all around the Throne shone a halo like an emerald rainbow. In a circle around the Throne there were twenty-four thrones and seated upon them twenty-four Elders dressed in white with golden crowns upon their heads. From the central Throne come flashes of lightning, noises and peals of thunder. Seven lamps are burning before the Throne, and they are the seven Spirits of God. In front of the Throne there appears a sea of glass as clear as crystal. On each side, encircling the Throne, are four Living Creatures covered with eyes in front and behind. The first Living Creature is like a lion, the second is like a calf, the third has a face like a man, and the fourth Living Creature appears like an eagle in flight. These four Creatures have each of them six wings and are covered with eyes, all around them, and even within them. Day and night they never cease to say,

"Holy, holy, holy is the Lord God, the Almighty, Who was and Who is and Who is coming."

THE CEASELESS WORSHIP OF HEAVEN

And whenever the Living Creatures give glory and honor 4
and thanksgiving to the One Who sits upon the Throne, 9
Who lives for timeless ages, the twenty-four Elders prostrate
themselves before Him Who is seated upon the Throne and
worship the One Who lives for timeless ages. They cast
their crowns before the Throne and say,

"Thou art worthy, O Lord our God, to receive glory
and honor and power, for Thou didst create all things; by
Thy Will they existed and were created."

THE SEALED BOOK OF FUTURE EVENTS

Then I noticed in the right hand of the One seated upon 5
the Throne a book filled with writing both inside and on its 1
back, and it was sealed with seven seals. And I saw a mighty
angel who called out in a loud voice,

"Who is fit to open the book and break its seals?"

And no one in Heaven or upon earth or under the earth
was able to open the book, or even to look at it. I began to
weep bitterly because no one could be found fit to open
the book, or even to look at it, when one of the Elders said
to me:

"Do not weep. See, the Lion from the tribe of Judah, the
Root of David, has won the victory and is able to open
the book and break its seven seals."

Then, standing in the very center of the Throne and of
the four Living Creatures and of the Elders, I saw a Lamb

that seemed to have been slaughtered. He had seven horns and seven eyes, which are the seven Spirits of God and are sent out into every corner of the earth. Then He came and took the book from the right hand of Him Who was seated upon the Throne.

THE NEW HYMN OF THE CREATED AND OF THE REDEEMED

5
8   When He had taken the book, the four Living Creatures and the twenty-four Elders prostrated themselves before the Lamb. Each of them had a harp, and they had golden bowls full of incense, which are the prayers of the saints. They sang a new song and these are the words they sang:

"Worthy art Thou to take the book and break its seals, for Thou hast been slain and by Thy blood hast purchased for God men from every tribe, and tongue, and people, and nation! Thou hast made them a kingdom of priests for our God, and they shall reign as kings upon the earth."

THE HYMN OF THE WHOLE COMPANY OF HEAVEN

5
11   Then in my vision I heard the voices of many angels encircling the Throne, the Living Creatures and the Elders. There were myriads of myriads and thousands of thousands, crying in a great voice,

"Worthy is the Lamb Who was slain, to receive power and riches and wisdom, and strength and honor and glory and blessing!"

Then I heard the voice of everything created in Heaven, upon earth, under the earth and upon the sea, and all that are in them saying,

"Blessing and honor and glory and power be given to Him Who sits upon the Throne, and to the Lamb, for timeless ages!"

The four Living Creatures said, "Amen," while the Elders
fell down and worshiped.

THE LAMB BREAKS THE SEALS

THE FIRST RIDER: CONQUEST

Then I watched while the Lamb broke one of the seven   6
seals, and I heard one of the four Living Creatures say in   1
a voice of thunder,
"Come out!"
I looked, and before my eyes was a white horse. Its rider
carried a bow, and he was given a crown. He rode out
conquering and bent on conquest.

THE SECOND RIDER: WAR

Then, when the Lamb broke the second seal, I heard the   6
second Living Creature cry,   3
"Come out!"
And another horse came forth, red in color. Its rider was
given power to deprive the earth of peace, so that men should
kill one another. A huge sword was put into his hand.

THE THIRD RIDER: FAMINE

When the Lamb broke the third seal, I heard the third   6
Living Creature say,   5
"Come out!"
I looked again and there before my eyes was a black horse.
Its rider had a pair of scales in his hand, and I heard a
voice which seemed to come from the four Living Creatures,
saying,
"A quart of wheat for a quarter, and three quarts of

barley for a quarter—but no tampering with the oil or the wine!"

THE FOURTH RIDER: DEATH

6
7   Then, when He broke the fourth seal I heard the voice of the fourth Living Creature cry,

"Come out!"

Again I looked, and there appeared a horse sickly green in color. The name of its rider was Death, and the Grave followed close behind him. A quarter of the earth was put into their power, to kill with the sword, by famine, by violence, and through the wild beasts of the earth.

THE CRY OF THE MARTYRS IN HEAVEN

6
9   When the Lamb broke the fifth seal, I could see, beneath the Altar, the souls of those who had been killed for the sake of the Word of God and through the faithfulness of their witness. They cried out in a loud voice, saying,

"How long shall it be, O Lord of All, holy and true, before Thou shalt judge and avenge our blood upon the inhabitants of the earth?"

Then each of them was given a white robe, and they were told to be patient a little longer, until the number of their fellow servants and of their brethren, who were to die as they had died, should be complete.

THE AWE-FULL WRATH OF GOD

6
12   Then I watched while He broke the sixth seal. There was a tremendous earthquake, the sun turned dark like coarse black cloth, and the full moon was red as blood. The stars of the sky fell upon the earth, just as a fig tree sheds unripe figs when shaken in a gale. The sky vanished as

though it were a scroll being rolled up, and every mountain
and island was jolted out of its place. Then the kings of the
earth, and the great men, the captains, the wealthy, the
powerful, and every man, whether slave or free, hid themselves in caves and among mountain rocks. They called out to
the mountains and the rocks:

"Fall down upon us and hide us from the Face of Him
Who sits upon the Throne, and from the wrath of the
Lamb! For the great day of their wrath has come, and who
can stand against it?"

JUDGMENT STAYED FOR THE SEALING OF GOD'S PEOPLE

Later I saw four angels standing at the four corners of   7
the earth holding in check the four winds of the earth that   1
none should blow upon the earth or upon the sea or upon
any tree. Then I saw another angel ascending out of the
east, holding the seal of the living God. He cried out in a
loud voice to the four angels who had the power to harm
the earth and the sea:

"Do no harm to the earth, nor to the sea, nor to the
trees until we have sealed the servants of our God upon
their foreheads."

I heard the number of those who were thus sealed and it
was 144,000, from every tribe of the sons of Israel. Twelve
thousand were sealed from the tribe of Judah; twelve thousand from the tribe of Reuben; twelve thousand from the
tribe of Gad; twelve thousand from the tribe of Asher;
twelve thousand from the tribe of Naphtali; twelve thousand from the tribe of Manasseh; twelve thousand from the
tribe of Simeon; twelve thousand from the tribe of Levi;
twelve thousand from the tribe of Issachar; twelve thousand
from the tribe of Zebulun; twelve thousand from the tribe

of Joseph; and twelve thousand were sealed from the tribe
of Benjamin.

THE COUNTLESS HOST OF THE REDEEMED

7
9   When this was done I looked again, and before my eyes
appeared a vast crowd beyond man's power to number.
They came from every nation and tribe and people and language, and they stood before the Throne of the Lamb,
dressed in white robes with palm branches in their hands.
They shouted with a great voice these words:

"Salvation belongs to our God Who sits upon the Throne
and to the Lamb!"

Then all the angels stood encircling the Throne, the Elders
and the four Living Creatures and prostrated themselves
with heads bowed before the Throne and worshiped God
saying,

"Amen! Blessing and glory and wisdom and thanksgiving
and honor and power and strength be given to our God for
timeless ages!"

THE COUNTLESS HOST EXPLAINED

7
13   Then one of the Elders addressed me and asked,
"These who are dressed in white robes—who are they,
and where do they come from?"

"You know, my Lord," I answered him.

Then he told me:

"These are those who have come through the Great
Oppression; they have washed their robes and made them
white in the blood of the Lamb. That is why they now
have their place before the Throne of God, and serve
Him day and night in His Temple. He Who sits upon the
Throne will be their Shelter. They will never again know

hunger or thirst. The sun shall never beat upon them, neither shall there be any scorching heat, for the Lamb Who is in the center of the Throne will be their Shepherd and will lead them to springs of Living Water. And God will wipe away every tear from their eyes."

THE SEVENTH SEAL: COMPLETE SILENCE

Then, when He had broken the seventh seal, there was utter silence in Heaven for what seemed to be about half an hour.

8

1

THE VISION OF THE SEVEN TRUMPETERS

Then I saw the seven angels who stand in the presence of God, and seven trumpets were put into their hands.

8

2

Then another angel came and stood by the Altar holding a golden censer. He was given a great quantity of incense to add to the prayers of all the saints, to be laid upon the golden Altar before the Throne. And the smoke of the incense rose up before God from the angel's hand, mingled with the prayers of the saints. Then the angel took the censer, filled it with fire from the Altar, and hurled it upon the earth. And at that there were thunderings and noises, flashes of lightning and an earthquake.

Then the seven angels who were holding the seven trumpets prepared to blow them.

THE FIRST TRUMPET: HAIL AND FIRE

The first angel blew his trumpet. Hail and fire mingled with blood appeared, and were hurled upon the earth. One-third of the earth was burned up, one-third of all the trees was burned up, and every blade of green grass was burned up.

8

7

THE SECOND TRUMPET: THE BLAZING MOUNTAIN

8
8   The second angel blew his trumpet, and something like
a vast mountain blazing with fire was thrown into the sea.
A third part of the sea turned into blood, a third of all live
creatures in the sea died, and a third part of all shipping
was destroyed.

THE THIRD TRUMPET: THE POISONOUS STAR

8
10   Then the third angel blew his trumpet and there fell
from the sky a huge star blazing like a torch. It fell upon a
third of the rivers and springs of water. The name of the
star is said to be Apsinthus (Wormwood). A third of all
the waters turned into wormwood, and many people died
because the waters had become so bitter.

THE FOURTH TRUMPET: LIGHT FROM THE SKY DIMINISHES

8
12   The fourth angel blew his trumpet, and a third part of
the sun, a third part of the moon and a third of the stars were
struck. A third part of the light of each of them was darkened,
so that light by day and light by night were both diminished
by a third part.

THE CRY OF PITY FROM MIDHEAVEN

8
13   Then in my vision I saw a solitary eagle* flying in midheaven, crying in a loud voice,

"Alas, alas, alas for the inhabitants of the earth, for there
are three more trumpet blasts which the three angels shall
sound!"

* Not "angel," as in K.J.V.

THE FIFTH TRUMPET: THE FATHOMLESS PIT

The fifth angel blew his trumpet. I saw a star that had 9
fallen down from Heaven to earth, and he was given the 1
key to the fathomless Pit. Then he opened the Pit, and
smoke like the smoke of a vast furnace rose out of it, so that
the light of the sun and the air itself grew dark from the
smoke of the Pit.

Then out of the smoke emerged locusts to descend upon
the earth. They were given powers like those of earthly
scorpions. They had orders to do no harm to any grass,
green thing or tree upon the earth, but only to injure those
human beings who did not bear the seal of God upon their
foreheads. They had no power to kill men, but only to torture
them for five months. The torture they could inflict was
like the pain of a scorpion's sting.

In those days men will seek death but they will never
find it; they will long to die but death will elude them. These
scorpions looked to me in my vision like horses prepared
for battle. On their heads were what appeared to be crowns
like gold; their faces were like human faces, and they had
long hair like women. Their teeth were like lions' teeth,
their breasts were like iron breastplates, and the noise of
their wings was like the noise of a host of chariots and
horses charging into battle. They have tails and stings like
scorpions, and it is in their tails that they possess the power
to injure men for five months. They have as their king
the angel of the Pit, whose name in Hebrew is Abaddon
and in Greek Apollyon (meaning the Destroyer).

The first Disaster is now past, but I see two more ap-
proaching.

THE SIXTH TRUMPET: THE DESTROYING ANGELS

9   Then the sixth angel blew his trumpet, and I heard a
13   solitary voice speaking from the four corners of the golden
Altar that stands in the presence of God. And it said to the
sixth angel who held the trumpet,

"Release the four angels who are bound at the great
river Euphrates!"

Then these four angels who had been held ready for the
hour, the day, the month and the year, were set free to kill
a third part of all mankind. The number of their horsemen
was two hundred million—I heard what their number was. In
my vision I saw these horses and their riders, and their
breastplates were fiery-red, blue and yellow. The horses'
heads looked to me like the heads of lions, and out of their
mouths poured fire and smoke and sulfur. A third of all
mankind died from the fearful effects of these three, the fire,
the smoke and the sulfur which pours out of their mouths.
For the power of these horses lies in their mouths and in
their tails. Indeed their tails are like serpents with heads,
and with these they inflict injury.

The rest of mankind, who did not die in this fearful
destruction, neither repented of the works of their own
hands nor ceased to worship evil powers and idols of gold,
silver, brass, stone, or wood, which can neither see nor hear
nor move. Neither did they repent of their murders, their
sorceries, their sexual sins, nor of their thieving.

THE ANGEL WITH THE LITTLE BOOK

10   Then I saw another mighty angel descending from Heav-
1   en. He was clothed in a cloud, and there was a rainbow

around his head. His face blazed like the sun, his legs like pillars of fire, and he had a little book lying open in his hand. He planted his right foot on the sea and his left foot on the land, and then shouted with a loud voice like the roar of a lion. And when he shouted the seven thunders lifted their voices. When the seven thunders had rolled I was on the point of writing but I heard a voice from Heaven, saying,

"Seal up what the seven thunders said, but do not write it down!"

Then the angel whom I had seen bestriding the sea and the land raised his right hand to Heaven and swore by the Living One of the timeless ages, Who created Heaven, earth and sea and all that is in them:

"There shall be no more delay! In the days which shall soon be announced by the trumpet blast of the seventh angel the Mysterious Purpose of God shall be completed, as He assured His servants the prophets."

Then the voice which I had heard from Heaven was again in my ears, saying,

"Go and take the little book which lies open in the hand of the angel whose feet are planted on both sea and land."

So I went off toward the angel, asking him to give me the little book.

"Take it," he said to me, "and eat it up. It will be bitter to your stomach, but sweet as honey in your mouth."

Then I took the little book from the angel's hand and swallowed it. It was as sweet as honey to the taste but when I had eaten it up it was bitter to my stomach.

JOHN IS INSTRUCTED TO PROPHESY

10   Then they said to me, "It is again your duty to prophesy
11   about many peoples, nations, languages and kings." And
I was given a measuring rod like a staff, and I was told: "Get
up and measure the Temple of God, and the Altar, and count
those who worship there. But leave out of your measurement
the courtyard outside the Temple—do not measure that
at all. For it has been given over to the nations, and they will
trample over the Holy City for forty-two months."

GOD'S TWO WITNESSES

11   "And I will give authority to My Two Witnesses to
3   proclaim the Message, clothed in sackcloth for twelve hundred and sixty days."

These are the two olive trees and the two lampstands
which stand before the Lord of the earth. If anyone tries
to harm them, fire issues from their mouths and consumes
their enemies. Indeed, if anyone should try to hurt them,
this is the way in which he will certainly meet his death.
These Witnesses have power to shut up the sky and stop
any rain from falling during the time of their preaching.
Moreover, they have power to turn the waters into blood,
and to strike the earth with any plague as often as they wish.

THE EMERGENCE OF THE ANIMAL

11   Then, when their work of witness is complete, the Ani-
7   mal will come up out of the Pit and go to war with
them. It will conquer and kill them, and their bodies will
lie in the street of the great City, which is called by those
with spiritual understanding, "Sodom" and "Egypt"—the
very place where their Lord Himself was crucified. For

three and a half days men from all peoples and tribes and languages and nations will gaze upon their bodies and will not allow them to be buried. The inhabitants of the earth will gloat over them and will hold celebrations and send one another presents, because these two prophets had brought such misery to the inhabitants of the earth.

THE RESURRECTION AND ASCENSION OF THE TWO WITNESSES

But after three and a half days the Spirit of Life from 11
God entered them and they stood upright on their feet. 11
This struck terror into the hearts of those who were watching them, and they heard a tremendous Voice speaking to these two from Heaven, saying,

"Come up here!"

And they went up to Heaven in a cloud in full view of their enemies. And at that moment there was a great earthquake, a tenth part of the City fell in ruins and seven thousand people were known to have been killed in the earthquake. The rest were terrified, and acknowledged the glory of the God of Heaven.

THE SEVENTH TRUMPET:

(i) THE WORSHIP OF HEAVEN

The second Disaster is now past, and I see the third Dis- 11
aster following hard upon the heels of the second. The 14
seventh angel blew his trumpet. There arose loud voices in Heaven and they were saying,

"The Kingship of the World now belongs to our Lord and to His Christ, and He shall be King for timeless ages!"

Then the twenty-four Elders, who sit upon their thrones in the presence of God, prostrated themselves and, with bowed heads, worshiped God, saying:

"We thank Thee, O Lord Who art God the Almighty, Who art and Who wast, that Thou hast assumed Thy great power and hast become King. The nations were full of fury, but now Thy wrath has come and with it the time for the dead to be judged and for reward to be given to Thy servants, the prophets and the saints, and all who fear Thy Name, both small and great. Now is the time for destroying the destroyers of the earth!"

Then the Temple of God in Heaven was thrown open and the Ark of His Agreement within His Temple could be clearly seen. Accompanying this sight were flashes of lightning, loud noises, peals of thunder, an earthquake and a violent storm of hail.

THE SEVENTH TRUMPET:
(ii) THE SIGN OF THE WOMAN

12
1 Then a huge sign became visible in the sky—the figure of a Woman clothed with the sun, with the moon under her feet and a crown of twelve stars upon her head. She was pregnant, and cried out in her labor and in the pains of bringing forth her child.

THE SEVENTH TRUMPET:
(iii) THE DRAGON, THE ENEMY OF THE WOMAN

12
3 Then another sign became visible in the sky, and I saw that it was a huge red Dragon with seven heads and ten horns, with a diadem upon each of his heads. His tail swept down a third of the stars in the sky and hurled them upon the earth. The Dragon took his place in front of the Woman who was about to give birth to a child, so that as soon as she did so he might devour it. She gave birth to a male child who is to shepherd all the nations "with a rod of iron."

Her child was snatched up to God and to His Throne, while the Woman fled into the desert where there was a place prepared for her by God's command. There they would take care of her for twelve hundred and sixty days.

WAR IN HEAVEN

Then war broke out in Heaven. Michael and his angels battled with the Dragon. The Dragon and his angels fought back, but they did not prevail and they were expelled from Heaven. So the huge Dragon, the Serpent of ancient times, who is called the Devil and Satan, the Deceiver of the whole world, was hurled down upon the earth, and his angels were hurled down with him.

12

7

THE VICTORY OF HEAVEN PROCLAIMED

Then I heard a great voice in Heaven cry:

"Now the salvation and the power and kingdom of our God, and the authority of His Christ, have come! For the Accuser of our brethren has been thrown down from his place, where he stood before our God accusing them day and night. Now they have conquered him through the blood of the Lamb, and through the Word to which they bore witness. They did not cherish life even in the face of death!

"Therefore, rejoice, O Heavens, and all you who live in the Heavens! But alas for the earth and the sea, for the Devil has come down to you in great fury, knowing that his time is short!"

12

10

THE DRAGON'S ENMITY AGAINST THE WOMAN

And when the Dragon saw that he had been cast down upon the earth, he began to pursue the Woman who had

12

13

given birth to the male child. But she was given two great eagle's wings so that she could fly to her place in the desert, where she is kept safe from the Serpent for a time and times and half a time. Then the Serpent ejected water from his mouth, streaming like a river in pursuit of the Woman, to drown her in its flood. But the earth came to the Woman's rescue, opened its mouth and swallowed up the river which the Dragon had emitted from his mouth. Then the Dragon raged with fury against the Woman and went off to make war against the rest of her children—those who keep the commandments of God and bear their witness to Jesus.

THE ANIMAL FROM THE SEA

12 Then, as I stood on the sand of the seashore, there rose
18 out of the sea before my eyes an Animal with seven heads and ten horns. There were diadems upon its horns and blasphemous names upon its heads. The Animal which I saw had the appearance of a leopard, though it had the feet of a bear and a mouth like the mouth of a lion. Then the Dragon gave it his own power and throne and great authority. One of its heads appeared to have been wounded to death but the mortal wound had healed.

The whole earth followed the Animal with wonder, and they worshiped the Dragon because he had given authority to the Animal. Then they worshiped the Animal, too, saying:

"Who is like the Animal? Who could make war against it?"

It was allowed to speak monstrous blasphemies and to exert its authority for forty-two months.

So it poured out blasphemies against God, blaspheming His Name and His Dwelling Place and those who live in Heaven. Moreover, it was permitted to make war upon the

saints and to conquer them; the authority given to it ex-
tended over every tribe and people and language and nation.
All the inhabitants of the earth will worship it—all those
whose names have not been written in the Book of Life
which belongs to the Lamb slain from the foundation of
the world.

PARENTHETICAL: A WORD TO THE READER

Let the listener hear this: 13

If any man is destined for captivity he will go into cap-   9
tivity. If any man kills with the sword he must himself be
killed with the sword. Amid all this stands the endurance and
faith of the saints.

THE ANIMAL FROM THE EARTH

Then I saw another Animal rising out of the earth, and it   13
had two horns like a lamb but it spoke in the voice of a   11
dragon. It uses the full authority of the first Animal in its
presence. It compels the earth and all its inhabitants to
worship the first Animal—the one with the mortal wound
which had healed. It performs great signs: before men's
eyes it makes fire fall down from heaven to earth. It deceives
the inhabitants of the earth by the signs which it is allowed
to perform in the presence of the Animal, and it tells them to
make a statue in honor of the Animal which received the
sword thrust and yet survived. Further, it was allowed to give
the breath of life to the statue of the Animal so that the
statue could speak and condemn to death all those who do
not worship its statue. Then it compels all, small and great,
rich and poor, free men and slaves, to receive a mark on their
right hands or on their foreheads. The purpose of this is
that no one should be able to buy or sell unless he bears the

mark of the name of the Animal or the number of its name. Understanding is needed here: let every thinking man calculate the number of the Animal. It is the number of a man, and its number is six hundred and sixty-six.*

THE VISION OF THE LAMB AND THE FIRST OF THE REDEEMED

14   Then I looked again and before my eyes the Lamb was
1   standing on Mount Sion, and with Him were a hundred and forty-four thousand who had His Name and His Father's Name written upon their foreheads. Then I heard a sound coming from Heaven like the roar of a great waterfall and the heavy rolling of thunder. Yet the sound which I heard was also like the music of harpists sweeping their strings. And now they are singing a new song of praise before the Throne, and before the four Living Creatures and the Elders. No one could learn that song except the one hundred and forty-four thousand who had been redeemed from the earth. These are the men who have never defiled themselves with women, for they are celibate. These are the men who follow the Lamb wherever He may go; these men have been redeemed from among mankind as first fruits to God and to the Lamb. They have never been guilty of any falsehood and they are beyond reproach.

THE ANGEL WITH THE GOSPEL

14   Then I saw another angel flying in midheaven, holding
6   the everlasting Gospel to proclaim to the inhabitants of the earth—to every nation and tribe and language and people. He was crying in a loud voice:

---

* This number undoubtedly refers to NERO CAESAR, by means of a simple Hebrew cipher. Guesses about its later application have been rife throughout the centuries. The triple six stands for a concentration of evil, six being the number of imperfection.

"Reverence God, and give glory to Him; for the hour of His Judgment has come! Worship Him Who made Heaven and earth, the sea and the springs of water."

THE ANGEL OF DOOM

Then another, a second angel, followed him crying: 14
Fallen, fallen is Babylon the Great! She who made all   8
nations drink the wine of her passionate unfaithfulness!"

THE ANGEL OF JUDGMENT

Then a third angel followed these two, crying in a loud   14
voice: 9
"If any man worships the Animal and its statue and bears its mark upon his forehead or upon his hand, then that man shall drink the wine of God's passion, poured undiluted into the cup of His Wrath. He shall be tortured by fire and sulfur in the presence of the Holy angels and of the Lamb. The smoke of such men's torture ascends for timeless ages, and there is no respite from it day or night. Such are the worshipers of the Animal and its statue, and among their number are all who bear the mark of its name."

THE CALL TO STAND FAST

In all this stands the endurance of the saints—those who   14
keep the commandments of God and their faith in Jesus.   12

THE SECURITY OF THE SAINTS

Then I heard a voice from Heaven, saying,   14
"Write this! From henceforth happy are the dead who   13
die in the Lord!"
"Happy indeed," says the Spirit, "for they rest from their labors and their deeds go with them!"

THE HARVEST OF GOD'S WRATH

14   Once again I looked, and a white cloud appeared before
14   me with someone sitting upon the cloud with the appearance
of a Man. He had a golden crown on his head, and held a
sharp sickle in his hand. Then another angel came out from
the Temple, calling in a loud voice to the one sitting on the
cloud,

"Thrust in your sickle and reap, for the time of reaping has
come and the harvest of the earth is fully ripe!"

Then the one sitting upon the cloud swung his
sickle upon the earth, and the reaping of the earth was
done.

Then another angel came out from the Temple in Heaven,
and he also had a sharp sickle. Yet another angel came out
from the Altar where he has command over the fire, and
called out in a loud voice to the angel with the sharp
sickle,

"Thrust in your sharp sickle and harvest the clusters from
the vineyard of the earth, for the grapes are fully
ripe!"

Then the angel swung his sickle upon the earth and
gathered the harvest of the earth's vineyard, and threw it
into the great winepress of the Wrath of God. The grapes
were trodden outside the City, and out of the winepress
flowed blood for two hundred miles in a stream as high as
the horses' bridles.

THE SEVEN LAST PLAGUES PREPARED

15   Then I saw another Sign in Heaven, vast and awe-inspir-
1   ing: seven angels are holding the seven last plagues, and with
these the Wrath of God is brought to an end.

THE HYMN OF THE REDEEMED

And I saw what appeared to be a sea of glass shot through 15
with fire, and upon this glassy sea were standing those who   2
had emerged victorious from the fight with the Animal, its
statue, and the number which denotes its name. In their
hands they hold harps which God has given them, and they
are singing the song of Moses the servant of God, and the
song of the Lamb, and these are the words they sing:

"Great and wonderful are Thy works, O Lord God, the
Almighty! Just and true are Thy ways, Thou King of the
nations! Who should not reverence Thee, O Lord, and
glorify Thy Name? For Thou alone art holy; therefore all
nations shall come and worship before Thee, for Thy just
judgments have been made plain!"

THE ANGELS LEAVE THE TEMPLE OF GOD—

Later in my vision I saw the Temple of the Tabernacle 15
of Testimony in Heaven wide open, and out of the Temple   5
came forth the seven angels who hold the seven plagues.
They were dressed in spotless shining linen, and they were
girded round their breasts with golden girdles.

Then one of the four Living Creatures gave to the seven
angels seven golden bowls filled with the Wrath of God
Who lives for timeless ages. The Temple was filled with
smoke from the glory and power of God, and no one could
enter the Temple until the seven plagues of the seven angels
were past and over.

—AND ARE ORDERED TO POUR OUT THE BOWLS OF HIS WRATH

Then I heard a loud voice from the Temple saying to the 16
seven angels,   1

"Go and pour out upon the earth the seven bowls of the Wrath of God!"

THE FIRST BOWL: ULCERS

16
2 The first angel went off and emptied his bowl upon the earth. Whereupon loathsome and malignant ulcers attacked all those who bore the mark of the Animal and worshiped its statue.

THE SECOND BOWL: DEATH IN THE SEA

16
3 The second angel emptied his bowl into the sea, which turned into a fluid like the blood of a corpse, and every living thing in it died.

THE THIRD BOWL: WATER BECOMES BLOOD

16
4 Then the third angel emptied his bowl into the rivers and springs of water, and they turned into blood. And I heard the angel of the waters say:

"Just art Thou in these Thy judgments, Thou Who art and wast the holy One! For they have spilled the blood of saints and prophets, and now Thou hast given them blood to drink. They have what they deserve."

And I heard the Altar say,

"Yes, O Lord, God Almighty, Thy judgments are true and right."

THE FOURTH BOWL: SCORCHING HEAT

16
8 The fourth angel emptied his bowl over the sun, and the sun was given power to scorch men in its fiery blaze. Then men were terribly burned in the heat, and they blasphemed the Name of God Who has control over these afflictions; but they neither repented nor gave Him glory.

THE FIFTH BOWL: THE PLAGUE OF DARKNESS

Then the fifth angel emptied his bowl upon the throne of the Animal. Its kingdom was plunged into darkness; men gnawed their tongues in agony, cursed the God of Heaven for their pain and their ulcers, but refused to repent of what they had done. 16 10

THE SIXTH BOWL: THE GREAT RIVER DRIED UP

Then the sixth angel emptied his bowl upon the great river Euphrates. The waters of that river were dried up to prepare a road for the kings from the East. And then I noticed three foul spirits, looking like frogs, emerging from the mouths of the Dragon, the Animal, and the False Prophet. They are diabolical spirits performing wonders and they set out to muster all the kings of the world for battle on the Great Day of God, the Almighty. 16 12

So they brought them together to the place called in Hebrew, Armageddon.*

THE WORDS IN THE BACKGROUND

"See, I am coming like a thief! Happy is the man who stays awake and keeps his clothes at his side, so that he will not have to walk naked and men see his shame." 16 15

THE SEVENTH BOWL: DEVASTATION FROM THE AIR

The seventh angel emptied his bowl into the air. A loud voice came out of the Temple, from the Throne, saying, "The End has come!" 16 17

Then followed flashes of lightning, noises and peals of

* Verse 16 has been put immediately before Verse 15, which seems to be its natural place.

thunder. There was a terrific earthquake, the like of which no man has ever seen since mankind began to live upon the earth—so great and tremendous was this earthquake. The Great City was split into three parts, and the cities of all the nations fell in ruins. And God called to mind Babylon the Great and made her drink the cup of the wine of His furious wrath. Every island fled and the mountains vanished. Great hailstones like heavy weights fell from the sky, and men blasphemed God for the curse of the hail, for it fell upon them with savage and fearful blows.

THE JUDGMENT OF THE EVIL WOMAN ANNOUNCED

17 Then came one of the seven angels who held the seven
1 bowls, and said to me:

"Come, and I will show you the judgment passed upon the great Harlot who is seated upon many waters. It is with her that the kings of the earth have debauched themselves and the inhabitants of the earth have become drunk on the wine of her filthiness."

THE GORGEOUS MOTHER OF EVIL

17 Then he carried me away in spirit into the desert. There
3 I saw a Woman riding upon a scarlet Animal, covered with blasphemous titles and having seven heads and ten horns. The Woman herself was dressed in purple and scarlet, glittering with gold, jewels and pearls. In her hand she held a golden cup full of the earth's filthiness and her own foul impurity. On her forehead is written a name with a secret meaning—BABYLON THE GREAT, MOTHER OF ALL HARLOTS AND OF THE EARTH'S ABOMINATIONS.

THE VISION EXPLAINED

Then I noticed that the Woman was drunk with the blood 17
of the saints and of the martyrs for Jesus. As I watched her,   6
I was filled with utter amazement, but the angel said to me:

"Why are you amazed? I will explain to you the mystery
of the Woman and of the Animal with seven heads and ten
horns which carries her. The Animal, which you saw, once
lived but now is no more—it will come up out of the Pit
only to meet with destruction. The inhabitants of the earth,
whose names have not been written in the Book of Life
from the foundation of the world, will be utterly astonished
when they see that the Animal was, and is not, and yet is to
come. (Here we need a mind with understanding.)

"The seven heads are seven hills on which the Woman
takes her seat. There are also seven kings; five have been
dethroned, one reigns, and the other has not yet appeared—
when he comes he must remain only for a short time. As
for the Animal which once lived but now lives no longer,
it is an eighth king which belongs to the seven, but it goes
to utter destruction. The ten horns which you saw are ten
kings who have not yet received their power to reign, but
they will receive authority to be kings for one hour in
company with the Animal. They are of one mind, and they
will hand over their power and authority to the Animal.
They will all go to war with the Lamb, and the Lamb, with
His called, chosen, and faithful followers, will conquer
them. For He is Lord of lords and King of kings."

Then he said to me:

"As for the waters which you saw, on which the Woman
took her seat, they are peoples and vast crowds, nations and
languages. The ten horns and the Animal which you saw

will loathe the Harlot, and leave her deserted and naked. Moreover, they will devour her flesh, and then consume her with fire. For God has put it into their hearts to carry out His Purpose by making them of one mind, and by handing over their authority to the Animal, until the Words of God have been fulfilled.

"The Woman that you saw is the Great City which dominates the kings of the earth."

THE FINAL OVERTHROW OF BABYLON

18   Later I saw another angel coming down from Heaven,
 1   armed with great authority. The earth shone with the splendor of his presence, and he cried in a mighty voice:

"Fallen, fallen is Babylon* the Great! She has become a haunt of devils, a prison for every unclean spirit, and a cage for every filthy and hateful bird. For all nations have drunk the wine of her passionate unfaithfulness and have fallen thereby. The kings of the earth have debauched themselves with her, and the merchants of the earth have grown rich from the extravagance of her dissipation!"

Then I heard another voice from Heaven, crying:

"Come out from her, O my people, lest you become accomplices in her sins and must share in her punishment. For her sins have mounted up to the sky, and God has remembered the tale of her wickedness. Pay her back in her own coin—yes, pay her back double for all that she has done! In the cup which she mixed for others mix her a drink of double strength! For the pride in which she flaunted herself give her torture and misery! Because she says to herself, 'Here I sit a queen on a throne; I am no woman who lacks

* Referring to Rome, but prophetically to any great, prosperous but Godless city.

a man and I shall never know sorrow!' So in a single day her punishments shall strike her—death, sorrow, and famine, and she shall be burned in the fire. For mighty is the Lord God Who judges her!"

THE LAMENT OVER THE CITY

Then the kings of the earth, who debauched and indulged 18 themselves with her, will wail and lament over her. Standing 9 at a safe distance through very fear of her torment, they will watch the smoke of her burning and cry,

"Alas, alas for the Great City, Babylon the mighty City, that your judgment should come in a single hour!"

The merchants of the earth shall also wail and lament over her, for there is no one left to buy their goods—cargoes of gold and silver, jewels and pearls, fine linen, purple, silk and scarlet, all kinds of scented wood, every sort of ivory vessel, every kind of vessel of precious wood, of bronze, iron and marble; cinnamon, spice, incense, myrrh, frankincense, wine, oil, fine flour and corn; cattle, sheep and horses; chariots, slaves, the very souls of men.

Those who bought and sold these things, who had gained 18 their wealth from her, will stand afar off through fear of 15* her punishment, weeping and lamenting and saying,

"Alas, alas for the Great City that was dressed in fine linen, purple and scarlet, and was bedecked with gold and jewels and pearls—alas that in a single hour all that wealth should be destroyed!"

Then every shipmaster and seafarer—sailors and all whose business is upon the sea—stood and watched the smoke of her burning from afar, and cried out,

* Verse 14 has been incorporated into Verse 23, which seems to be its natural place.

"What city was ever like the Great City?"

They even threw dust on their heads and cried aloud as they wept, saying:

"Alas, alas for the Great City where all who had ships on the sea grew wealthy through the richness of her treasure! Alas that in a single hour she should be ruined!"

A COMMENT IN THE BACKGROUND

18   "Rejoice over her fate, O Heaven, and all you saints,
20 apostles, and prophets! For God has pronounced His Judgment for you against her!"

THE WORDS OF BABYLON'S DOOM

18   Then a mighty angel lifted up a stone like a huge mill-
21 stone and hurled it into the sea, saying:

"So shall Babylon the Great City be sent hurtling down to disappear for ever! Never more shall the sound of harpists and musicians, flute players and trumpeters be heard in you again! Never again shall a craftsman of any craft be found in you; never again will the sound of the millstone's grinding be heard in you! No light of a lamp shall ever shine in you again, and the voices of bridegroom and bride shall be heard in you no more! The fruit of your soul's desire is lost to you for ever. All your luxuries and brilliance are lost to you and men will never find them in you again!

"For your merchants were the great ones of the earth, and all nations were seduced by your witchery!"

For in her was discovered the blood of prophets and saints, indeed, the blood of all who were ever slaughtered upon the earth.

REJOICING IN HEAVEN

Afterward I heard what sounded like the mighty roar of 19
a vast crowd in Heaven crying: 1

"Alleluia! Salvation and glory and power belong to our
God, for His judgments are true and just. He has judged the
great Harlot who corrupted the earth with her wickedness,
and He has avenged upon her the blood of His servants!"

Then they cried a second time,

"Alleluia! The smoke of her destruction ascends for timeless ages!"

Then the twenty-four Elders and the four Living Creatures
prostrated themselves and worshiped God Who is seated
upon the Throne, saying,

"Amen, Alleluia!"

Then out of the Throne came a voice, saying,

"Praise our God, all you who serve Him, all you who reverence Him, both small and great!"

And then I heard a sound like the voices of a vast crowd,
the roar of a great waterfall and the rolling of heavy thunder,
and they were saying:

"Alleluia! For the Lord our God, the Almighty, has come
into His Kingdom! Let us rejoice, let us be glad with all our
hearts. Let us give Him the glory, for the Wedding Day of
the Lamb has come, and His Bride has made herself ready.
She may be seen dressed in linen, gleaming and spotless—
for such linen is the righteous living of the saints!"

INSTRUCTION TO JOHN

Then he said to me,   19

"Write this down: Happy are those who are invited to   9

the Wedding Feast of the Lamb!"

Then he added,

"These are true words of God."

At that I fell at his feet to worship him, but he said to me,

"No! I am your fellow servant and fellow servant with your brothers who are holding fast their witness to Jesus. Give your worship to God!"

(This witness to Jesus inspires all prophecy.)

THE WORD OF GOD ON THE WHITE HORSE

19
11
Then I saw Heaven wide open, and before my eyes appeared a white horse, whose rider is called Faithful and True, for His judgment and His warfare are just. His eyes are a flame of fire and there are many diadems upon His head. There is a Name written upon Him, known only to Himself. He is dressed in a cloak dipped in blood, and the Name by which He is known is the Word of God.

The armies of Heaven follow Him, riding upon white horses and clad in white and spotless linen. Out of His mouth there comes a sharp sword with which to strike the nations. He will shepherd them "with a rod of iron," and alone He will tread the winepress of the furious wrath of God the Almighty. Written upon His cloak and upon His thigh is the Name KING OF KINGS AND LORD OF LORDS.

THE FEAST OF DEATH AFTER BATTLE

19
17
Then I saw an angel standing alone in the blazing light of the sun, and he shouted in a loud voice, calling to all the birds flying in mid-air:

"Come, flock together to God's great feast! Here you may eat the flesh of kings and captains, the flesh of strong men, of horses and their riders—the flesh of all men, free men and slaves, small and great!"

And I saw the Animal with the kings of the earth and their armies massed together for battle against the Rider upon the horse and His army. The Animal was captured and with it the False Prophet who had performed marvels in its presence, which he had used to deceive those who accepted the mark of the Animal and worshiped its statue. These two were thrown alive into the Lake of Fire which burns with sulfur.

The rest were killed by the sword which issues from the mouth of the Rider upon the horse; and all the birds gorged themselves on their flesh.

SATAN BOUND FOR A THOUSAND YEARS

Then I saw an angel coming down from Heaven with the 20 key of the Pit and a huge chain in his hand. He seized the 1 Dragon, the Serpent of ancient days, who is both the Devil and Satan, and bound him fast for a thousand years. Then he hurled him into the Pit, and locked and sealed it over his head, so that he could deceive the nations no more until the thousand years were past. But then he must be set free for a little while.

THE FIRST RESURRECTION

And I saw thrones, with appointed judges seated upon 20 them. Then I saw the souls of those who had been executed 4 for their witness to Jesus and for proclaiming the Word of God—those who never worshiped the Animal or its statue, and had not accepted its mark upon their foreheads or their hands. They came to life and reigned with Christ for a thousand years. (The rest of the dead did not come to life until the thousand years were over.) This is the First Resurrection. Happy and holy is the one who shares in the First Resurrection! The Second Death cannot touch such men; they shall be priests of God and of Christ, and shall reign with Him for the thousand years.

SATAN FINALLY DESTROYED

20 Then, when the thousand years are over, Satan will be
7 released from his prison, and will set out to deceive the nations in the four corners of the earth, Gog and Magog, and to lead them into battle. They will be as numerous as the sand of the seashore.

They came up and spread over the breadth of the earth; they encircled the army of the saints defending the Beloved City. But fire came down from the sky and consumed them. The Devil who deceived them was hurled into the Lake of Fire and Sulfur to join the Animal and the False Prophet. And there they shall be tortured day and night for timeless ages.

THE FINAL JUDGMENT

20 And then I saw a great white Throne, and One seated
11 upon it from Whose Presence both earth and sky fled and vanished.

Then I saw the dead, great and small, standing before the Throne, and the books were opened. And another book was opened, which is the Book of Life. And the dead were judged by what was written in the books concerning what they had done. The sea gave up its dead, and Death and the Grave gave up the dead which were in them. And men were judged, each according to what he had done.

Then Death and the Grave were themselves hurled into the Lake of Fire, which is the Second Death. If anyone's name was not found written in the Book of Life he was thrown into the Lake of Fire.

*   *   *

ALL THINGS MADE NEW

Then I saw a new Heaven and a new earth, for the first 21 Heaven and the first earth had disappeared, and the sea was 1 no more. I saw the Holy City, the New Jerusalem descending from God out of Heaven, prepared as a Bride dressed in beauty for her husband. Then I heard a great voice from the Throne crying:

"See! The Home of God is with men, and He will live among them. They shall be His people, and God Himself shall be with them, and will wipe away every tear from their eyes. Death shall be no more, and never again shall there be sorrow or crying or pain. For all those former things are past and gone."

Then He Who is seated upon the Throne said,

"See, I am making all things new!"

And He added,

"Write this down, for my words are true and to be trusted."

Then He said to me:

"It is done! I am Alpha and Omega, the Beginning and the End. I will give to the thirsty water without price from the Fountain of Life. The victorious shall inherit these things, and I will be God to him and he will be son to Me. But as for the cowards, the faithless and the corrupt, the murderers, the traffickers in sex and drugs, the worshipers of idols and all liars—their inheritance is in the Lake which burns with fire and sulfur, which is the Second Death."

THE VISION OF THE NEW JERUSALEM

21   Then one of the seven angels who hold the seven bowls
9   which were filled with the seven last plagues came to me and said,

"Come, and I will show you the Bride, the Wife of the Lamb."

Then he carried me away in spirit to the top of a vast mountain, and pointed out to me the City, the Holy Jerusalem, descending from God out of Heaven, radiant with the glory of God. Her brilliance sparkled like a very precious jewel with the clear light of crystal. Around her she had a vast and lofty wall in which were twelve gateways with twelve angels at the gates. There were twelve names inscribed over the twelve gateways, and they are the names of the twelve tribes of the sons of Israel. On the east there were three gateways, on the north three gateways, on the south three gateways and on the west three gateways. The wall of the City had twelve foundation stones and on these were engraved the names of the twelve Apostles of the Lamb.

THE MEASUREMENT OF THE CITY

21   The one who was talking to me had a golden rod in his
15   hand with which to measure the City, its gateways and its wall. The City lies foursquare, its length equal to its breadth. He measured the City with his rod, and it was twelve thousand furlongs in each direction, for its length, breadth,

and height are all equal. Then he measured its wall, and found that to be one hundred and forty-four half-yards high by human measurement (which the angel was using).

THE SPLENDOR OF THE CITY'S BUILDING

The wall itself was built of translucent stone, while the 21 City was of purest gold, with the brilliance of glass. The 18 foundation stones of the wall of the City were fashioned out of every kind of precious stone. The first foundation stone was jasper, the second sapphire, the third agate, the fourth emerald, the fifth onyx, the sixth cornelian, the seventh gold-stone, the eighth beryl, the ninth topaz, the tenth green gold-stone, the eleventh zircon, and the twelfth amethyst. The twelve gates were twelve pearls, each gate made of a single pearl. The street of the City was purest gold, gleaming like glass.

THE SPLENDOR WITHIN THE CITY

I could see no Temple in the City, for the Lord, the 21 Almighty God, and the Lamb are Themselves its Temple. 22 The City has no need for the light of sun or moon, for the splendor of God fills it with light, and its radiance is the Lamb. The nations will walk by its light, and the kings of the earth will bring their glory into it. The City's gates shall stand open day after day—and there will be no night there. Into the City they will bring the splendors and honors of the nations.

But nothing unclean, no one who deals in filthiness and lies, shall ever at any time enter it—only those whose names are written in the Lamb's Book of Life.

A FURTHER GLIMPSE OF THE CITY

22   Then he showed me the river of the Water of Life,
1 sparkling like crystal as it flowed from the Throne of
God and of the Lamb. In the middle of the street of the
City and on either bank of the river grew the Tree of Life,
bearing twelve fruits, a different kind for each month. The
leaves of the Tree were for the healing of the nations.

Nothing that has cursed mankind shall exist any longer;
the Throne of God and of the Lamb shall be within the
City. His servants shall worship Him; they shall see His
Face, and His Name will be upon their foreheads. Night
shall be no more; they have no more need for either lamp-
light or sunlight, for the Lord God will shed His Light
upon them and they shall reign as kings for timeless ages.

THE ANGEL ENDORSES THE REVELATION

22   Then the angel said to me:
6   "These words are true and to be trusted, for the Lord
God, Who inspired the prophets, has sent His angel to show
His servants what must shortly happen.

"See, I come quickly! Happy is the man who pays heed
to the words of the prophecy in this book."

JOHN'S PERSONAL ENDORSEMENT

22   It is I, John, who have heard and seen these things. At
8 the time when I heard and saw them I fell at the feet of the
angel who showed them to me and I was about to worship
him. But he said to me,

"No! I am fellow servant to you and to your brothers,
to the prophets and to those who keep the words of this
book. Give your worship to God!"

Then he added:

"Do not seal up the words of the prophecy in this book, for the time of their fulfillment is near. Let the wicked man continue his wickedness and the filthy man his filthiness; let the good man continue his good deeds and the holy man continue in holiness."

THE INTERJECTED WORDS OF CHRIST

"See, I come quickly! I carry My reward with Me, and repay every man according to his deeds. I am Alpha and Omega, the First and the Last, the Beginning and the End. Happy are those who wash their robes, for they have the right to the Tree of Life and the freedom of the gates of the City. Shut out from the City shall be the depraved, the sorcerers, the impure, the murderers and the idolaters, and everyone who loves and practices a lie!

"I, Jesus, have sent My angel to you with this Testimony for the Churches. I am both the Root and Stock of David, and the bright Star of the morning!"

THE INVITATION OF THE CHURCH AND THE SPIRIT

The Spirit and the Bride say, "Come!"

Let everyone who hears this also say, "Come!"

Let the thirsty man come, and let everyone who wishes take the Water of Life as a gift.

JOHN'S TESTIMONY TO THIS BOOK

Now I bear solemn witness to every man who hears the words of prophecy in this book:

If anyone adds to these words, God will add to him the disasters described in this book; if anyone takes away from the words of prophecy in this book, God will take away

from him his share in the Tree of Life and in the Holy City
which are described in this book.

He Who is Witness to all this says,

"Yes, I am coming very quickly!"

"Amen, come, Lord Jesus!"

The grace of the Lord Jesus be with all His people.

SUGGESTED BOOKS FOR
FURTHER STUDY

Commentaries on The Book of Revelation

I. T. Beckwith, THE APOCALYPSE OF JOHN
(The Macmillan Company)

A. W. Burnet, THE LORD REIGNETH
(Charles Scribner's Sons)

S. J. Case, THE REVELATION OF JOHN:
A HISTORICAL INTERPRETATION
(University of Chicago Press)

C. R. Erdman, THE REVELATION OF JOHN
(The Westminster Press)

M. Kiddle, THE REVELATION OF ST. JOHN
(The Moffatt New Testament Commentary)
(Harper & Brothers)

R. H. Preston, A. T. Hanson, THE REVELATION OF
ST. JOHN THE DIVINE
(Torch Bible Commentaries)
(The Macmillan Company)

H. F. Rall, MODERN PREMILLENNIALISM AND
THE CHRISTIAN HOPE
(Abingdon Press)

E. F. Scott, THE BOOK OF REVELATION
(Charles Scribner's Sons)

M. Rist, L. H. Hough, COMMENTARY ON
     REVELATION
     (Vol. XII, Interpreter's Bible)
     (Abingdon Press)

And the relevant sections in the following:

PEAKE'S COMMENTARY ON THE BIBLE
     (Thomas Nelson and Sons)

CONCISE BIBLE COMMENTARY,
     W. K. Lowther Clarke
     (The Macmillan Company)

A NEW COMMENTARY ON HOLY SCRIPTURE,
     C. Gore, H. L. Goudge, and A. Guillaume
     (The Macmillan Company)

INTRODUCING THE NEW TESTAMENT,
     A. M. Hunter
     (The Westminster Press)

AN INTRODUCTION TO THE NEW
     TESTAMENT, W. G. Robinson
     (St. Martin's Press, Inc.)